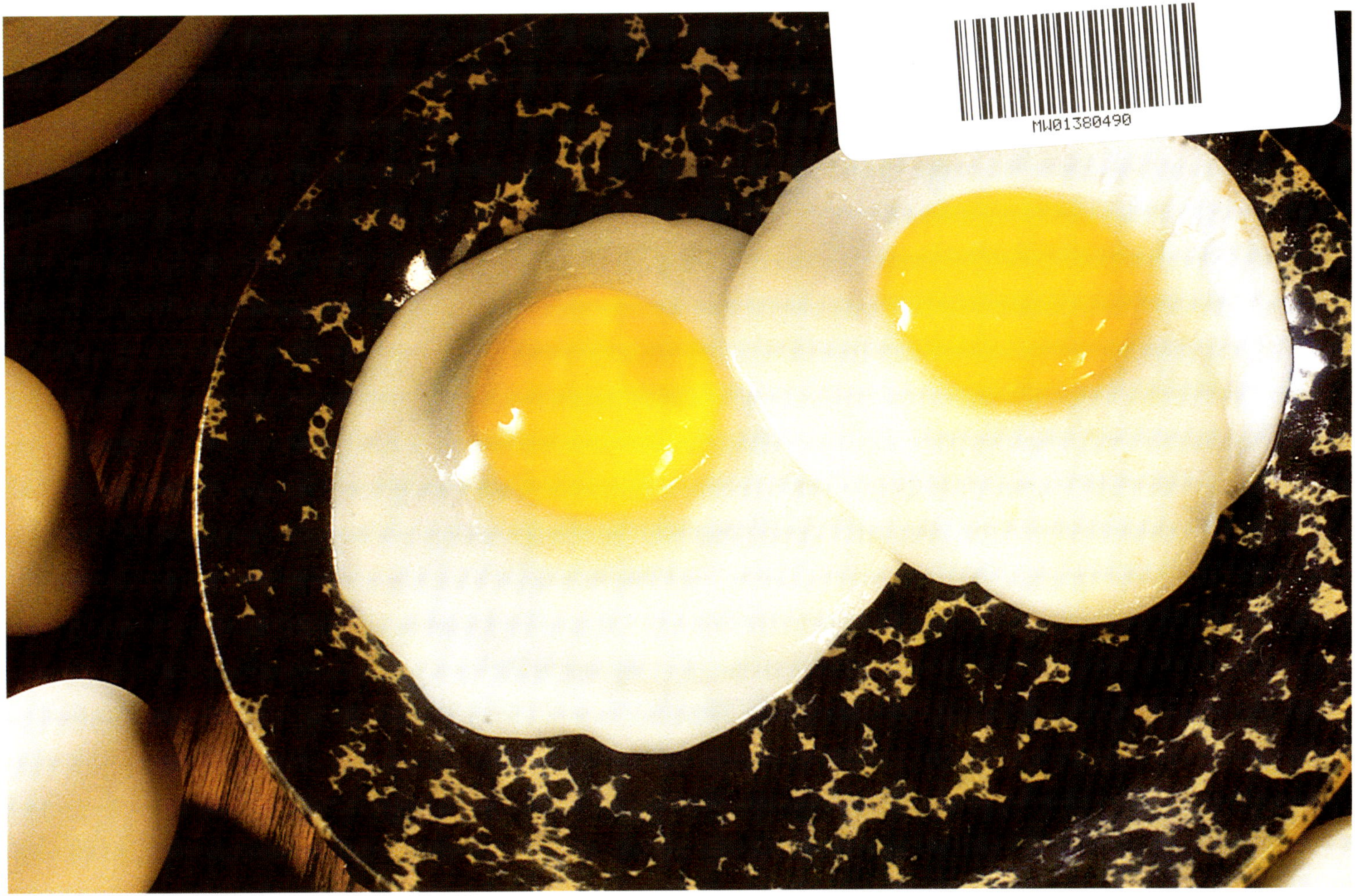

eggs

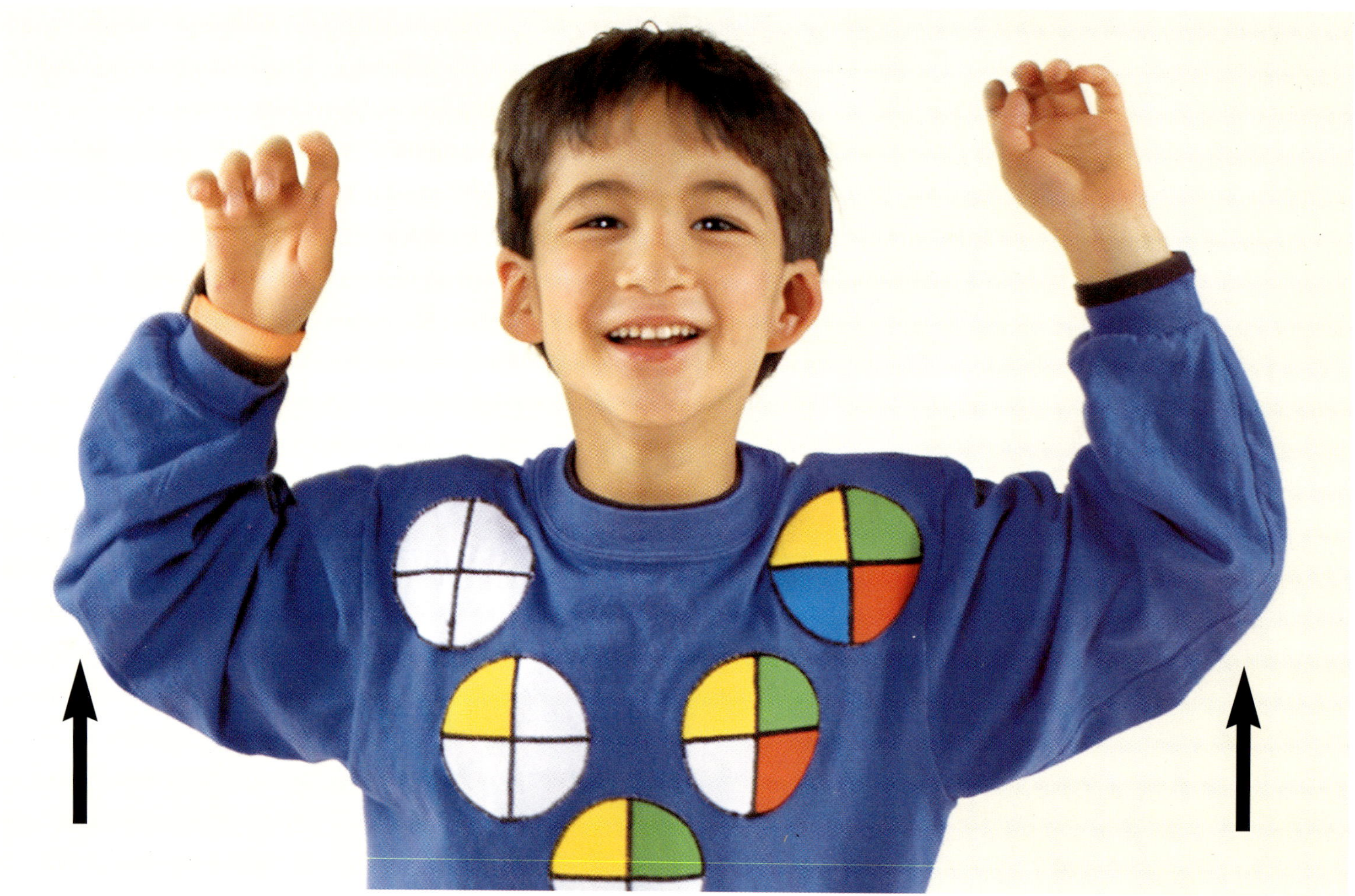

elbows

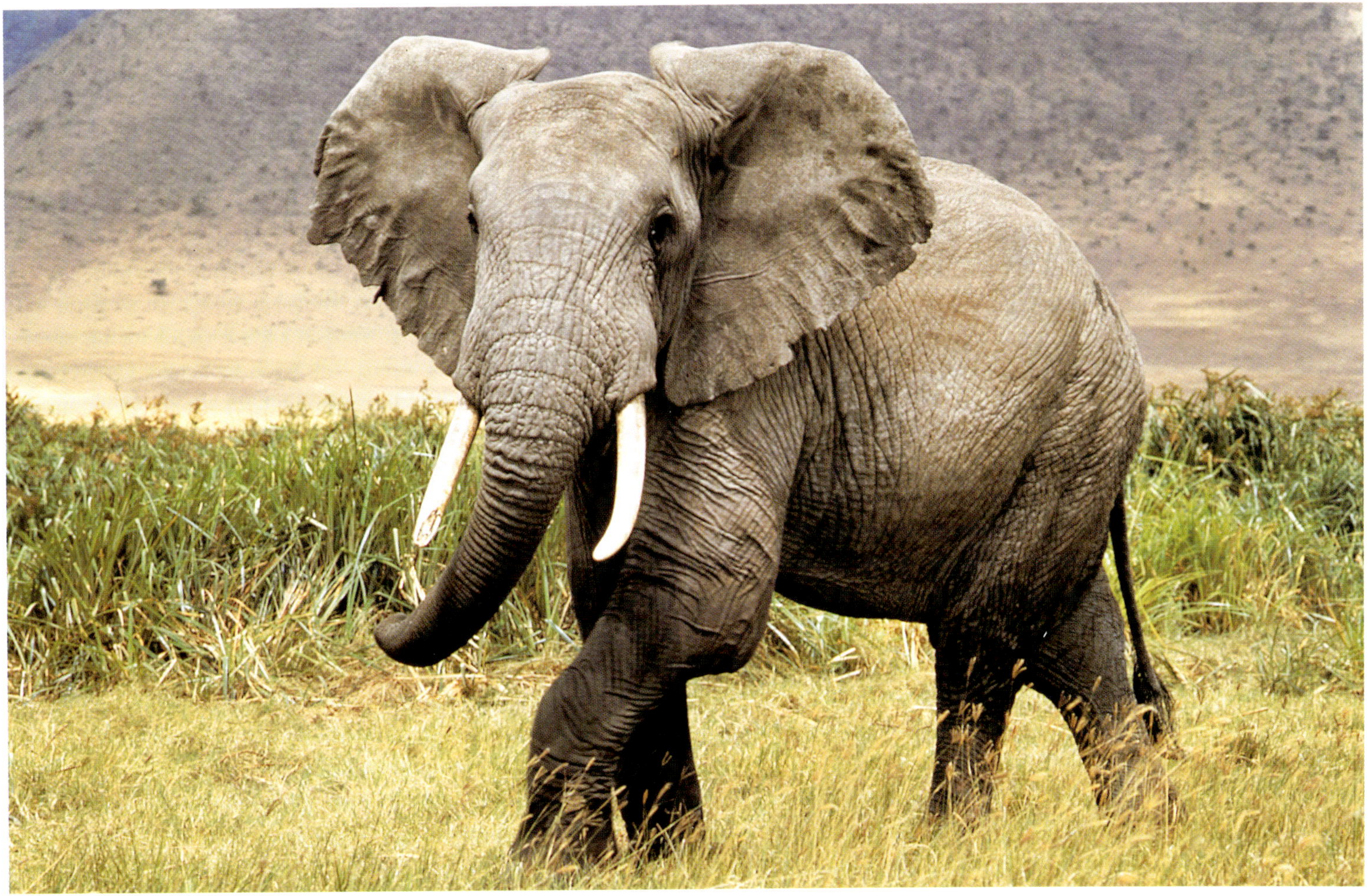

elephant

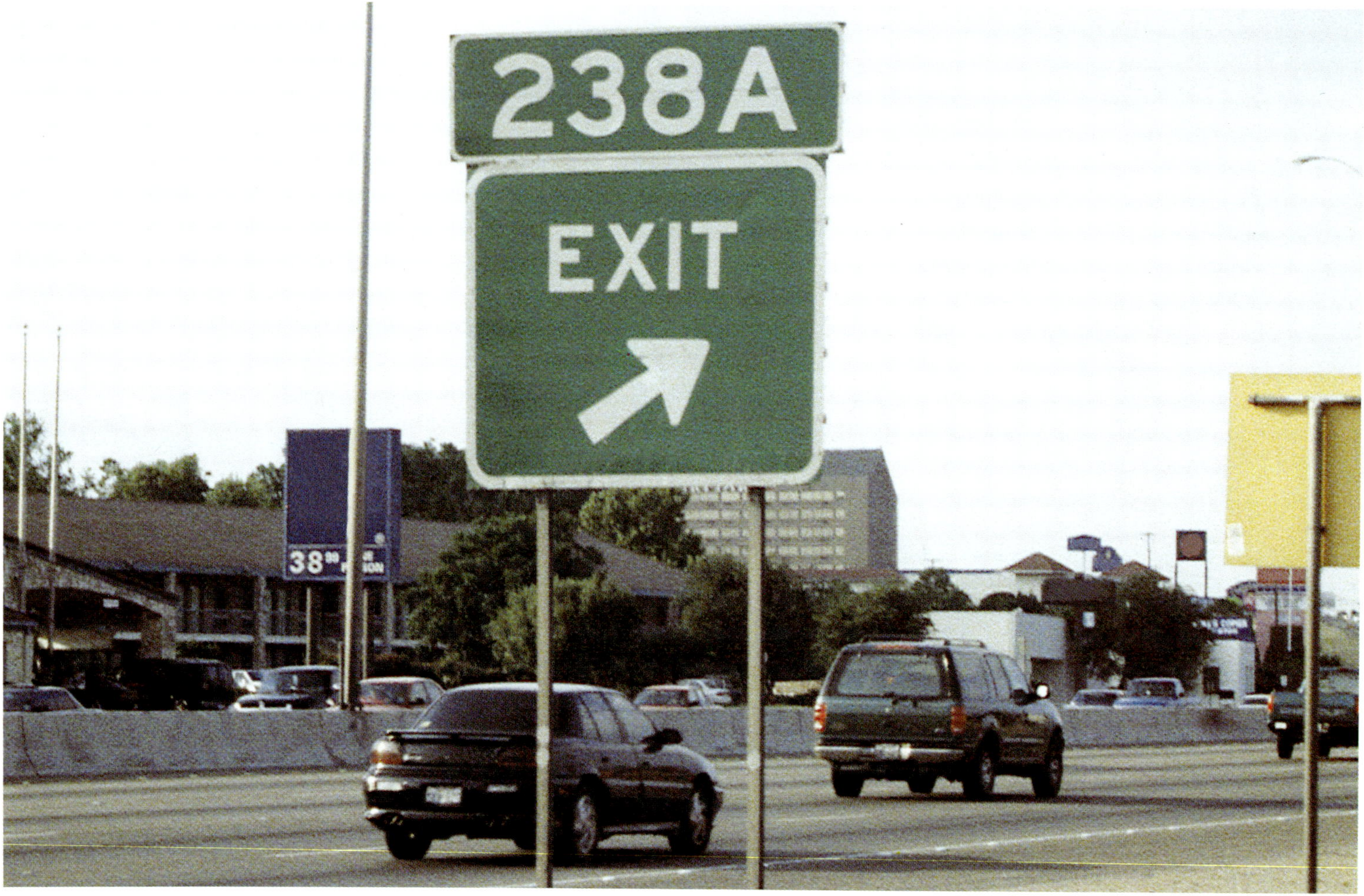

exit

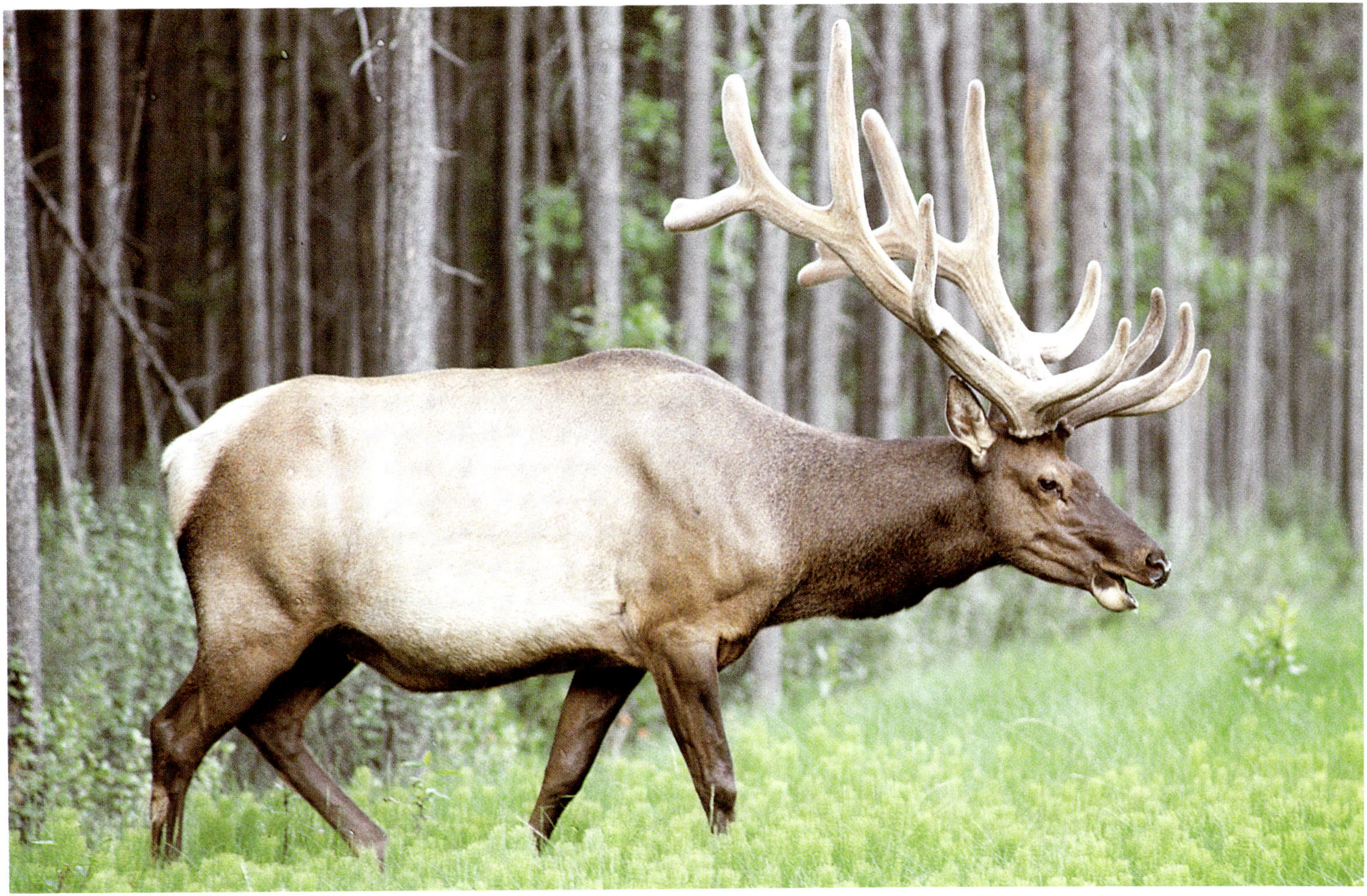

elk

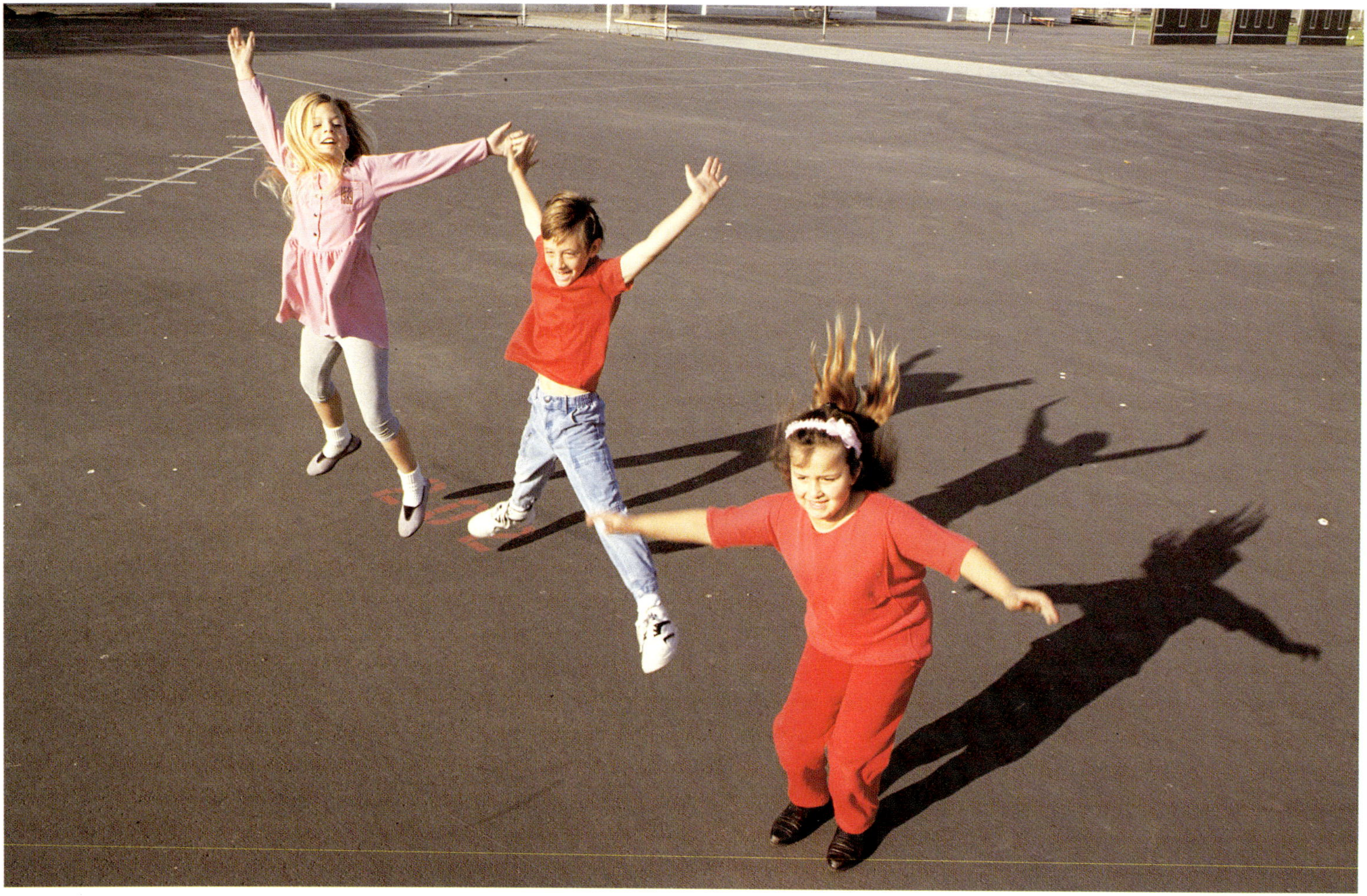

exercise

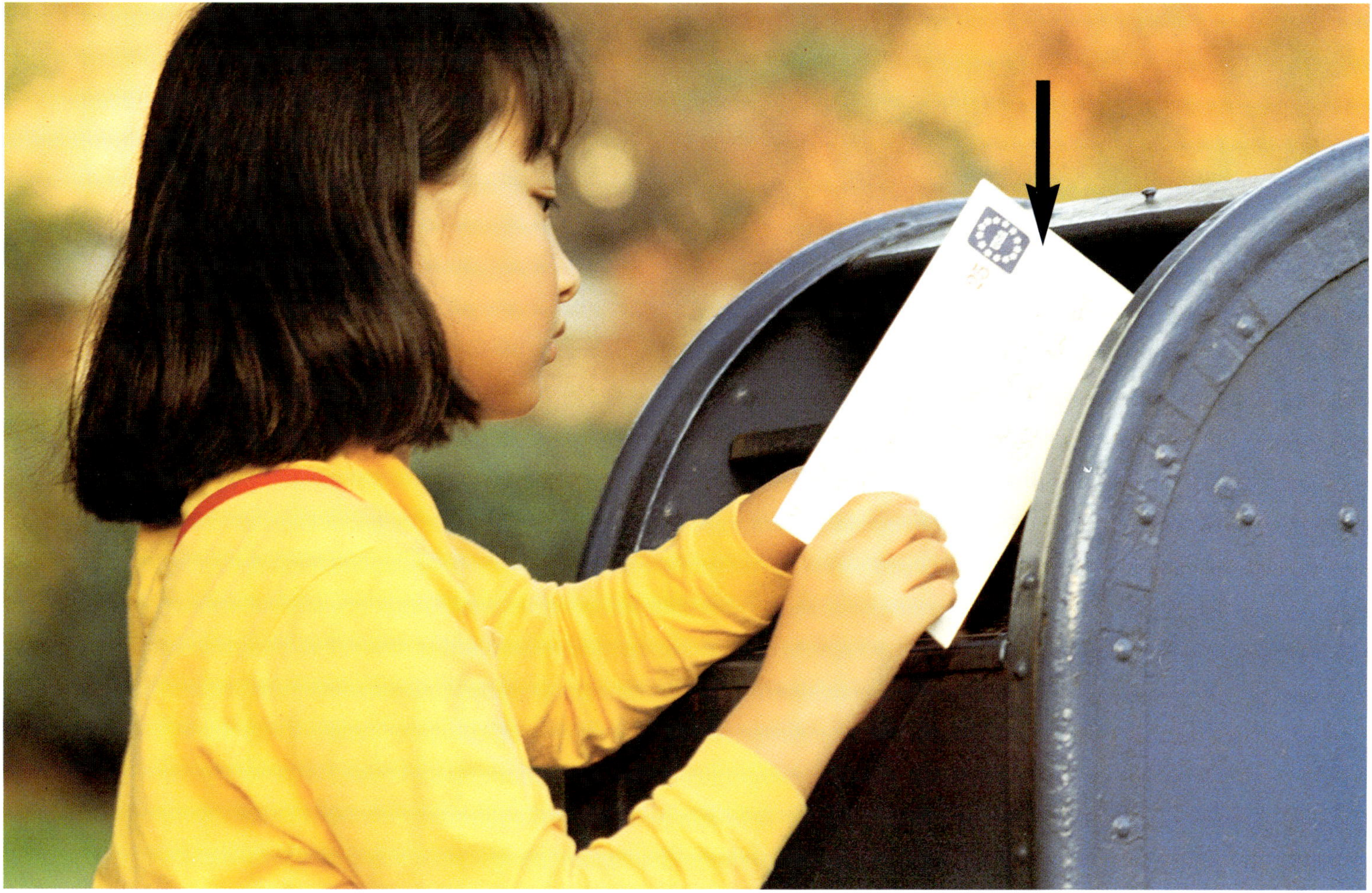

envelope

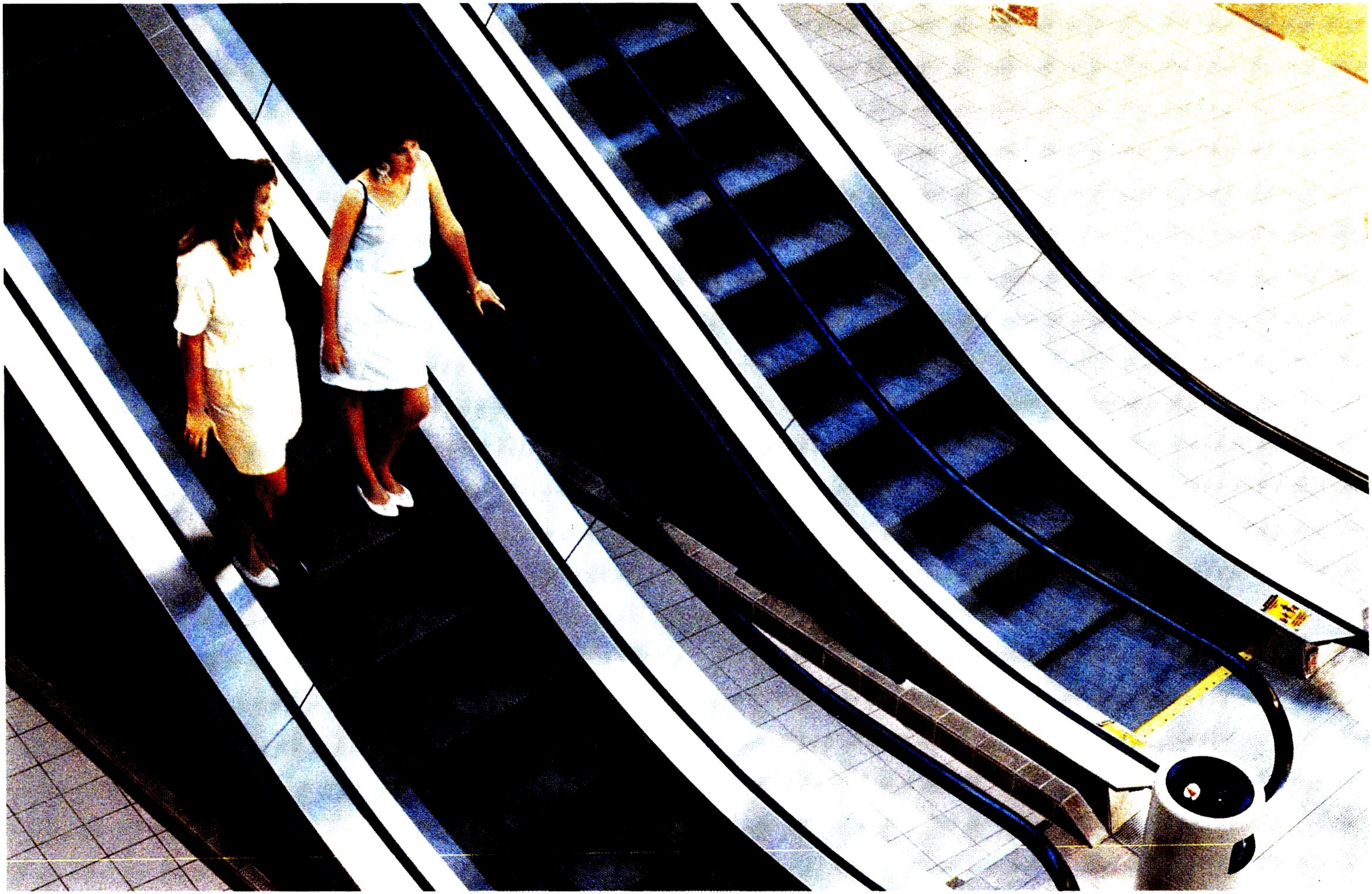

escalator